Liberty

How America's increasingly Socialist agenda impacts us all

Kevin Connolly

Liberty: The impact of government intervention in your life

By Kevin Connolly

ISBN 978-0-9847903-2-6

Where the people fear the government you have tyranny. Where the government fears the people you have liberty.

~ John Basil Barnhill

Contents

Foreword

There was a dream that was the United States of America, in which people would be free to determine their own path through life, their own needs and wants, and indeed, their own destiny. In this dream, individual liberty would be the basic moral principle of society, and law would be designed only to guarantee the people as much freedom as possible.

Human nature cannot fundamentally change. By instinct, we are greedy, self-righteous creatures who will look out for our own self-interest above all other priorities. Our founders understood that, and designed a government that would use our own nature to the advantage of the people. This government would be constitutionally limited in its power and scope, and its sole purpose would be to ensure the freedom of its people. This design is the very basis for our prosperity.

This design is based on the concept of Natural Law, which I'll go into further detail on later. The basic idea is that a human is *born free*, and can do whatever they please, until someone comes along and prevents those actions by force. In this case, that someone is Congress, and it's their job to manage law at the Federal level. Being born free, a law can only reduce our otherwise total freedom. Every law we pass takes away a little of our freedom. The more laws we have, the less free we are. America has *millions* of laws.

In other words, freedom is the *default* position, and governments are the sole source of restrictions of those freedoms. Governments do not grant freedoms; they can merely restrict or remove them. The Constitution does not grant us freedoms; it merely acknowledges some of the ones that were already there and guarantees that some of them can never be taken away.

As decreed in the 10th amendment to the Constitution, *the powers not delegated to the United States by the Constitution, nor prohibited by the States, are reserved to the States respectively, or to the people*. What that means is that if the Constitution does not explicitly grant a power to the Federal Government, then the Federal Government doesn't have that power and it is then left to the States to decide. If the States do not deny their people a power, then the people have that power. The genius of the 10th amendment is that if you don't like the laws in your state, you can move to another state. This ingenious design doesn't work when things are done at the federal level. You lose the right to choose; the freedom to decide.

Title I, Section 8 of the Constitution is designed implicitly to limit the size and scope of the Federal Government, thus allowing states and the people the maximum possible flexibility and freedom in deciding on the issues for themselves. Unfortunately, it seems the leaders of all three branches have stopped obeying the Constitution. The Federal Government has ballooned far beyond the size our founders intended, and has metastasized itself so malignantly and deeply into our lives that it may never be possible to treat it.

The Federal Government paid for all this Orwellian control over our lives by enacting the Income Tax in 1913 with the 16th Amendment to the Constitution. The 1918 Federal Budget authorized \$12.7B in outlays and took in \$3.6B in receipts (taxes). The FY2013 Federal Budget authorizes \$3.8T in outlays and takes in \$2.9T. In short, the government has multiplied itself 300 times (not inflation adjusted) in size in under a century, and its deficit has increased proportionally. On average, it nearly triples every year.

Gradually, the Income Tax has paid for more and more programs. As people are born and die, a growing number of citizens accept it as "The way things are". A century of people born under the Income Tax has desensitized us to the unchecked growth, violations of our Constitution and freedom, and other evils it delivers.

In order to understand the motivations behind this specific economic solution, you must first understand the Libertarian agenda. To understand Libertarianism, you must first understand Natural Law. Once you understand Natural Law, you will understand what America was designed to be. To that end, I shall explain those concepts before going into the actual budget in future books.

Any time you take money from one group of people and give it to another group of people, that's a form of Socialism known as Redistribution of Wealth. It's evil, it's unnatural, and it's un-American. Somewhere along the line of American history, society decided it was everyone's job to take care of people who couldn't or wouldn't take care of themselves. This has been an increasingly prevalent pattern since 1913, and especially since 1936; and it's ruining this country.

There was a time when accepting help from others was seen as a form of weakness and failure on the part of the provider. As Americans, it is both our tradition and our solemn natural duty to ensure self-sufficiency and provide for ourselves and our families. We must return to that method of thinking if we are ever to recover from our increasingly Socialist way of conducting our society.

There was a dream that was the United States of America. Can anyone remember it anymore?

Natural Law

Introduction

Natural Law is a system by which law is determined by nature. We use it to analyze ourselves and take morals and ethics from the very basis of human nature itself. The United States of America being founded on this concept, it is imperative that we understand it and its implications. First, I must show that the USA was indeed founded on this concept; then I can demonstrate what this means to us.

The Organic Law of 2007 cites the Declaration of Independence as official law, as there were some who disputed its lawfulness, being enacted prior to the Constitution and thus the Congress; and to include it within the United States Code, adopted in 1926.

Declaration of Independence

Analyze the wording of the Declaration of Independence, and the subsequent Constitution. Even the least astute reader will quickly realize the meaning thereof, as the wording was intentionally explicit.

> *We hold these truths to be self-evident, that all men are created equal, that they are endowed by their Creator with certain unalienable Rights, that among these are Life, Liberty and the pursuit of Happiness.*

"*We hold these truths*"– not these opinions, not this consensus, not this gentlemen's agreement. These are truths that are, by definition, absolutely and irrevocably true. They cannot be disputed, and they cannot be undone.

"To be self-evident"—these truths are so obvious that it seems silly that they even need to be said. Unfortunately, there was a series of tyrant Kings in a faraway land who just didn't seem to get the idea. We didn't create these truths; we don't authorize them; we merely recognize that they are already there. These rights are self-evident because anyone in any society can figure them out for themselves, and because they were here before we were.

"That all men are created equal"—Human rights have come a long way, and we've accepted this to mean all people. All people are created equal; that is, at the moment of our birth, none of us is any better or any worse than any other. We are equal under the law, and equal under the eyes of our Creator. What we do after that is up to us.

"That they are endowed by their creator"—Call it God, call it Nature, call it whatever you want. Whatever force created us has endowed us; has given to us as our Birthright...

"with certain unalienable Rights"— Not these privileges, not these temporary licenses. *Rights* – Certain actions which we fundamentally must be allowed to do. Certain rights which no mortal power may deny us.

"That among these are life, liberty, and the pursuit of happiness"— Every human has a right to live. Every human has a right to liberty. Every human has a right to pursue happiness.

No mere document, no King, no Constitution; indeed, no human faculty of any kind can grant these rights. They preexist; they are our God-given birthright; they are immortal. They come from a higher authority, and thus they are unalienable.

> *That to secure these rights, Governments are instituted among Men, deriving their just powers from the consent of the governed*

If you believe you have a birthright to something, it makes sense to organize like-minded people; to work together to ensure these rights are never taken away. Fulfilling this guarantee is the **only** purpose of Government.

Government's powers are derived from the people it governs. Not from the States; not from the Corporations; not from God; not from the might of our armies; not even from the Constitution. The people consent to delegate to the government its powers, and the people can take them away by withdrawing our consent.

> *That whenever any Form of Government becomes destructive of these ends, it is the Right of the People to alter or to abolish it*

Humans are imperfect creatures, and thus all our creations are imperfect. Our founders recognized that government in any form can deliver tyranny, and that the people maintain a right to fix that tyranny. We can do so by altering the government in question, or by abolishing it. The Government clearly has no interest in this today, as the destruction of these rights is in the best interest of a tyrant; thus it is the people who must take responsibility.

> *and to institute new Government, laying its foundation on such principles and organizing its powers in such*

form, as to them shall seem most likely to effect their Safety and Happiness.

If the people act on their right and go so far as to institute new government, it is further their right to design such government in a way that they think will provide them the best safety and happiness. Clearly, the purpose of such government is to protect the aforementioned unalienable rights from tyrants – Both present and future. It is the position of most Libertarians that the Federal Government has grown unconstitutionally into such a tyrant.

Enumerated Infractions of a Tyrant

Jefferson went on to enumerate the myriad infractions of the King, including:

He has dissolved Representative Houses repeatedly, for opposing with manly firmness his invasions on the rights of the people.

Houses of Representatives, similar to ours today, existed with representatives of the people of the colonies. The King dissolved these houses, paramount to the Super-Congress we saw recently.

He has refused for a long time, after such dissolutions, to cause others to be elected, whereby the Legislative Powers, incapable of Annihilation, have returned to the People at large for their exercise; the State remaining in the mean time exposed to all the dangers of invasion from without, and convulsions within.

He has prevented the free election of representatives. In this case there were none after such dissolution, but this can be easily compared with the lack of congressional term limits. Much as such lack exposed dangers to the people, today's corrupt congressmen pose such a danger to us; removable only through resignation or impeachment, both of which are nearly impossible to accomplish. As recently as 1995, the Supreme Court ruled that states cannot impose term limits upon their federal Representatives or Senators.

Constitutional amendment proposals have been brought forth to the Congress to impose such term limits upon themselves. As one would expect from any tyrant, they have all failed. I believe such a motion could pass only if the sitting body were exempted thereof, an unfortunate but obvious reflection upon our own history.

> *He has made Judges dependent on his Will alone for the tenure of their offices, and the amount and payment of their salaries.*

Judges could work through the King's permission only, and he directly decided if and what they were paid. Clearly he could impose his will upon our justice system through manipulation thereof. Supreme Court Justices are chosen *only* by the President. Of course, such President chooses such justices as agree with his agenda.

> *He has erected a multitude of New Offices, and sent hither swarms of Officers to harass our people and eat out their substance.*

Taxes! The King created a great number of new government jobs and offices to oversee and harass us. Today, the DoD alone employs over 3,000,000 people. Out of every hundred people in America, one works directly for the military. The Government eats out our substance, not by raiding our kitchens, but by raiding our wallets through taxation, and eating our freedoms by passing such laws as the Patriot Act.

One of the King's greatest infractions against us and humanity in general was the Stamp Act, which allowed British agents to write their own search warrants so they could ensure that every document in your home and on your person bore a taxed and purchased stamp with an image of the King on it. The Patriot Act allows Federal agents to write their own search warrants in exactly this same manner.

> *He has affected to render the Military independent of and superior to the Civil Power.*

The King assumed direct control over the military, and refused to let the people or our representatives decide where and how they were used. Congress hasn't declared a war since World War 2. Since then, Presidents have illegally and unconstitutionally sent our military to fight in Korea, Vietnam, Cuba, Iraq, Afghanistan, Pakistan, and countless other places. Not one of these wars was declared by Congress, as required by the Constitution.

> *He has combined with others to subject us to a jurisdiction foreign to our constitution, and unacknowledged by our laws; giving his Assent to their Acts of pretended Legislation*

The King, in concert with others, imposed his will upon us with utter disregard for the Constitution we had been working under at the time. If we read the 10th amendment to the Constitution, as I outlined earlier, any power not explicitly granted to the government by the Constitution is left to the States and the people. There is not one word about federally controlled education, agriculture, or environmental protection. There is not one word about socialized retirement, healthcare, medicine, food, or housing.

> *For imposing Taxes on us without our Consent*

We're all familiar with the idea of taxation without representation, but I have to wonder how many of us voted for the taxes we have today: Individual income tax, corporate income tax, social security payroll tax, Medicare payroll tax, unemployment insurance, "other retirement receipts", excise taxes, estate and gift taxes, customs duties, and 28 new taxes we are told will be delivered by Obamacare. The Federal Reserve, by artificially fiddling with interest rates, has incidentally imposed what we know as the Inflation Tax. That is, if you have a dollar now, and you hold on to it for 50 years, it won't be worth as much. By devaluing your dollar, you have effectively less money.

> *For depriving us in many cases, of the benefit of Trial by Jury*

The CIA and the President occasionally assassinate American Citizens with no trial under the guise of National Security, often citing the unconstitutional Patriot Act as their source of authority. A clear and repeated violation of the 5th and 6th amendments to the Constitution.

> *For taking away our Charters, abolishing our most valuable Laws and altering fundamentally the Forms of our Governments*

A colonial charter is a document that gives colonies legal status. This manipulation and abuse of his power caused the colonial governments to operate in a fundamentally different way. Today, we have the Patriot Act, Super Congress, and a Supreme Court that thinks it has the authority to make law. Congress has delegated to the Our government has been fundamentally altered in form.

> *He is at this time transporting large Armies of foreign Mercenaries to compleat the works of death, desolation, and tyranny, already begun with circumstances of Cruelty & Perfidy scarcely paralleled in the most barbarous ages, and totally unworthy the Head of a civilized nation.*

Look at the Occupy movement. In Crowds of legally assembled protestors got a little out of hand and were grossly overreacted to by the government with chemical weapons (tear gas) and large, high velocity projectiles (bean bags). We have seen this same situation unfold time and time again, with the Civil Rights movements for blacks and women, for protests against prohibition and war, and countless other times throughout our history.

In nearly every instance, the people persevered and eventually won major victories. The worst factor is that these are battles that should never have been needed in the first place. These people fight for freedom, and freedom is the most basic tenant of what makes America, America.

Constitution of the United States

> *We the People of the United States, in Order to form a more perfect Union, establish Justice, insure domestic Tranquility, provide for the common defence, promote the general Welfare, and secure the Blessings of Liberty to ourselves and our Posterity, do ordain and establish this Constitution for the United States of America.*

Everything you need to know about American Exceptionalism is right there in the Preamble. Here, the framers are introducing the Constitution and explaining its purpose, but it also explains what makes America special.

"We the People of the United States"—The Constitution was ordained and established by the People. Not some preexisting power; not a team of missionaries from the King or the Church; not a group of guys who had all the guns; not even a duly elected Congress; We the People. Many different Constitutions were tried; this is the one that the states finally (mostly) agreed upon. It was a consensus among the people, which would unite the several states.

"In order to form a more perfect Union"—The Colonies had gone through several different types of government over the course of colonization and expansion. They had tried many times to create a union in one form or another, and none of them lasted.

"establish Justice"—After many generations of tyranny and oppression, and the suppression of what seemed like the most basic of human rights, the Colonies were ready to run their own system of Justice, free from the King. The colonies believed in a higher form of justice; one that protects our rights and does not succumb to the whim of a tyrant.

"provide for the common defence"—The colonies had basically been a disparate group of largely independent city-states, and recognized that in working together they would be stronger. They also realized that if we decided to tell the King we were going to live our own way and under our own authority, there would be a great need to defend all that we were working so hard to create.

"insure domestic Tranquility"—Since the colonies were defining their own process of law and order, they must have a way to protect and defend them. Peace within the United States.

"promote the general Welfare"— To allow we the people to benefit from the justice, defense, and tranquility of the more perfect union.

"and secure the Blessings of Liberty to ourselves and our Posterity"—Our forefathers had fought very hard and very recently to obtain and secure their liberty, and they didn't want it whisked away again by a clearly superior military force.

"do ordain and establish this Constitution for the United States of America"—The requisite closing to explain exactly what the document is doing, to name the document, and indeed to reiterate the name of the newly formed nation. To explain the newly united nature of the several states. The use of "ordain" reiterates the idea that our rights are granted by a higher power. The use of "establish" shows that it overrules the failed attempts that came before. The use of "for" shows that the ultimate purpose of the Constitution is to serve the nation, not to rule over it.

Article I, Section 8 enumerates the specific powers of Congress, and ends by granting Congress the authority to make laws “necessary and proper” for executing those specific enumerated powers, or those granted by the Constitution, or “any department or officer” of the Federal Government.

> *To make all Laws which shall be necessary and proper for carrying into Execution the foregoing Powers, and all other Powers vested by this Constitution in the Government of the United States, or in any Department or Officer thereof.*

Clearly the purpose here was to limit the power of Congress to pass only those laws which are needed to let the Government do the job laid out in the Constitution.

Unfortunately to this end, Presidents have created whole departments and many “officers” whose power Congress may then pass law based on the necessity thereof. Article V even allows Congress to invent its own ways to ratify amendments, and the Congress can even create its own officers. Obviously, this was a flawed document, but it’s the best we could do with all the disagreement among the States.

During the debates regarding the adoption of the Constitution, its opponents repeatedly exclaimed that the Constitution as drafted would invite tyranny by the Federal Government. With the British violations of our rights so fresh in their minds, they demanded a Bill of Rights to enumerate the immunities of individual citizens. The opposition pointed out that the government’s powers were explicit and the peoples’ powers were myriad, and that enumeration of any specific rights would imply otherwise.

Bill of Rights

The Bill of Rights was created because several states complained that the rights of the people were explained too implicitly; that without explicitly delineating specific rights, those rights might be "misconstructed or abused".

Examine the wording of the Bill of Rights:

> *"Congress shall make no law..."*
> *"Shall not be infringed"*
> *"Shall not be violated"*
> *"No warrants shall issue"*
> *"No person shall be held to answer"*

I believe the 9th and 10th amendments to be among the most important, and to be the two which most clearly define America's basis in Natural Law:

> 9th: *"The enumeration in the Constitution, of certain rights, shall not be construed to deny or disparage others retained by the people."*
> 10th: *"The powers not delegated to the United States by the Constitution, nor prohibited by it to the States, are reserved to the States respectively, or to the people."*

Conclusion

Clearly, America was founded on Natural Law. Tyranny is the imposition of a leader's will upon the people. The two are mutually exclusive and cannot coexist without the inevitability of violent conflict. Our founders understood this, and thus they designed the Constitution specifically to limit the size and power of the Federal Government.

The 9th amendment clearly and explicitly explains that rights don't have to be enumerated by the Constitution to be rights. The 10th amendment tells us that the states may assume all powers not explicitly delegated to the Federal Government by the Constitution, and that any powers not thereby assumed by those states lie with the people.

In short, you are free to do whatever you please until the State or the Congress passes a law making it illegal. **Freedom is the default position;** the very definition of Natural Law.

Now that I have verbosely proven the basis of the United States upon Natural Law, it shall be fairly simple to show its application. Freedom is the default. Laws cannot grant freedoms, because we already have all freedoms until otherwise legislated. Laws can only take freedoms away. By that logic, the more laws we have, the less free we are.

Article I, Section 4 of the Constitution requires that *"the Congress shall assemble at least once in every year"*, implying that it was not intended to be a full-time job. There was a time when we didn't have career politicians. When not in session, Congressmen would go about their regular jobs. There was no retirement package, and there was no benefits package. You would come in, serve your time, and go back to your trade. As a result, only true statesmen would take on the additional burden of running the nation's business. We would do well to return to such a clean model.

Reading these several documents, it is very evident that our forefathers intended a small, frugal, responsible federal government, just large enough to provide those things which were enumerated in the Constitution. They did not intend a massive, all-controlling *state* with millions of people in its employ and its tentacles in every aspect of our lives.

Libertarianism

There are many conflicting definitions of Libertarianism. In this context, I will be discussing the interpretation of Right-Libertarianism and the Libertarian Party, which advocates Minarchism, Cultural Liberalism, Non-Interventionism, Constitutionalism, and Cultural Liberalism. Basically, we want the government to be small and the people to be free.

There is a distinct delineation between Libertarianism and Anarchism. Libertarianism demands small government in accordance with the Constitution. Anarchism demands no government. It's important to keep that distinction in mind.

To understand the Federal Government, one must first understand the principles upon which the government was created. Libertarianism is a political extension of Natural Law. Libertarians believe that personal liberty is the fundamental moral principle of society. It advocates strict limits to the size and scope of government and its activity, and maximizes individual liberty and freedom. Libertarianism is the very embodiment of what America was supposed to be.

> *Rightful liberty is unobstructed action according to our will within limits drawn around us by the equal rights of others. I do not add 'within the limits of the law' because law is often but the tyrant's will, and always so when it violates the rights of the individual.*
>
> *~ Thomas Jefferson*

"Unobstructed action according to our will"—is doing whatever we want, with no outside interference.

"Drawn around us by the equal rights of others"—our rightful liberty is limited only by the equal rights of others. In other words, do whatever you want, as long as you don't infringe upon anyone else's rights.

Jefferson goes on to explain that human rights outweigh the law. Clearly, he recognizes that our rights come from a higher authority. Furthermore, he explains that law is always the tyrant's will when it violates the rights of the individual. Clearly, Jefferson believed that law should not infringe upon our God-given birthrights. To the astute reader, it is clear by his language that Jefferson was exercising these beliefs when he wrote the Declaration of Independence.

Fundamental Concepts

Constitutionalism – If it's not in the Constitution, the federal government has no business meddling in it. It says so right there in Article I, Section 8, and again in the 9th and 10th amendments. The Constitution is our highest law, above all others. To disregard one part of it is to disregard the entire document, and thus the very fabric of America. It is the supreme law of the land. It is the manifesto of our founders' intentions. It is written in stone. Our elected officials swear an oath to uphold it, and doing so hasn't been the pattern in a long time.

Small Government – The smaller government is, the less it costs to run. The less it costs to run, the less it needs to tax. The less it taxes, the more of our money we can keep; the more employees a company can afford to hire. The less government regulates, the easier it is to do *everything*.

Government does not grant rights to people; people delegate some of their power to the government. Adherence to the Constitution that the states ratified is a condition of this delegation of powers. The Constitution lists all of the powers the federal government holds, and it is not allowed to stray beyond those *enumerated powers*.

Low Taxes – Initially, we were able to pay our way with a customs duty. Then we added a land tax, then an excise tax on liquor. As time goes on and the government grows, we add more and more taxes. We didn't even have an income tax until 1913. Since then, we've added taxes on cigarettes, gasoline, and every other product you could imagine.

We need to reduce the government to levels authorized by the Constitution, pay off our debt, and then eliminate and reduce as many taxes as possible. The ideal tax system is none at all.

Individual Liberty – As I've explained in great detail, the rights of the people should trump everything else. Protecting these rights is the main purpose in seceding from Britain, and the **only** purpose of having a government in the first place. It says so in the Declaration of Independence.

Clearly there will be cases where two freedoms are mutually exclusive; such as my right to smoke a cigarette versus your right not to be subjected to secondhand smoke. In these cases, regulation should tend to favor liberty; freedom of choice. If it cannot do so, it should ignore the issue and let the states handle it per the 10th amendment. If government would merely get out of the economy, the economy would fix itself.

Non-Interventionism – America was not meant to be the world's police force. If it's none of our business, we have no business meddling in it. Unconstitutional new-age ethics aside, we can't afford the warmongering that has pervaded our foreign policy over the past century.

The Constitution defines very clearly when we should go to war and that only the Congress may declare it. War should be declared every time, by the Congress. If the people so choose, we should conduct our war quickly and efficiently. Personally, I'd be in favor of keeping the spoils, such as Iraq.

Antisocialism – Any time you take money from someone and give it to someone else, that's socialism. Any redistribution of wealth is a form of socialism. America is about making it on your own through your own skills and merits. The increasingly prevalent welfare state is ruining this country.

Deregulation – Regulation causes overhead and waste. It forces companies to jump through hoops and hurdles, and forces them to replace productive people with bureaucrats. Regulation should exist only to protect those freedoms guaranteed to us by our Constitution, such as Life and Liberty. Some estimates put the number of regulations at 81,000 pages, at a cost of $1.75 Trillion per year. If we eliminated these regulations, we could effectively add that number directly to the Gross Domestic Product.

Free Enterprise – The market will correct itself, if only the government would butt out and allow it to do so. One of the reasons for our original secession was that the Crown kept poking its nose into our trading and it interfered with the economy, driving our traders and other businessmen to bankruptcy in many cases.

American Sovereignty - The Constitution decrees that all treaties duly signed are the "supreme law of the land", other provisions of the Constitution notwithstanding. Therefore we must be very careful in our choosing of treaties, and should prefer fewer to more. In the words of Thomas Jefferson:

Peace, commerce, and honest friendship with all nations, entangling alliances with none.

NATO and the United Nations are the two most entangling alliances in American history. I support withdrawing from NATO, thus obsoleting all security investments therein. Eliminate and save $264 Million in SIP alone.

In every case, services provided by private organizations are better than those provided by governments. Governments can take your money at gunpoint. Businesses have to convince you. If you don't like one company, you can go to a competitor. This option makes every transaction cleaner, more efficient, and cheaper. This is not the case with governments.

The government is not a bank. It is not an investor. It is not an insurance company. It is not a loyal advisor whose advice you can trust. Government intervention makes everything worse for everyone involved. If your business model is not profitable on its own virtue, the economy will show that. Business model viability should not be interfered with; it's dangerous, and on a large scale, it leads to recessions or worse.

Any time the government functions as a bank or an insurance company, it takes profitable business away from a company that could provide such function in the private sector. Taking a rightfully private job function and moving it into the government is a step toward totalitarianism and fascism.

No Foreign Aid – When you provide something to another country for a long period of time, they eventually become dependent on that aid. The longer it continues, the worse the dependency. Iraq will never be strong until we let them rule themselves completely. Israel will never be strong until they learn to supply and defend themselves again. Furthermore, with the sole exception of war cast upon us, the affairs of foreign countries are none of our business.

Finally, we need to fix our own problems before we can even consider fixing those of other countries, assuming we were actually fixing the problems at all. Foreign relations be damned;

if a relationship with another country isn't yielding us the same return as what we put into it, then it's not worth it.

No Grants - Giving money in the form of grants doesn't just generate new cash out of thin air; it has to come from somewhere. The government can't give you anything without first taking it away from someone else; and that someone is all of us. Eliminate all federal grants; states can tax their own people for their own programs, if their state legislatures so choose, given the *consent of the governed.*

Private Property – If you own land, then you have sovereign power over that land. You rule your land, more or less, supreme. You can defend it against trespassers, and you can decide who you want to allow onto that land. It then follows that if you offer a product or service on your property, then you should be able to decide who you want to offer those products and services to. The government shouldn't be allowed to force any of these decisions upon you.

Free Trade – Allow products and services to traffic freely and naturally between the US and other countries. Do not embargo them, do not sanction them, and do not subsidize them.

Separation of Powers – Cities should tax their own citizens to run their own programs. If the city cannot afford a program, they should not rely on the higher level governments to obtain funding. This would only remove funds from the areas that ran their governments responsibly. Counties and states should run the same way, taxing their citizens as they require to run their own programs, and not to send to lower levels. If your city can tax you to pay for a local police force, there is no need to tax the rest of the state just to pay for your city's needs. It stands to reason that this logic extends to the federal level as well.

Taxation and programs should be administered at the lowest possible level.

Legislative and Judicial Abuse of the Interstate Commerce Clause

Regulation as we know it today makes government bigger and more expensive. Regulation literally means "To keep regular"; Congress has the power to keep commerce regular. In all things, the Interstate Commerce Clause (Article I, Section 8, Clause 3) defines the authority of the Congress to regulate:

> *[The Congress shall have Power] To regulate Commerce with foreign Nations, and among the several States, and with the Indian tribes;*

The Supreme Court decreed in *Gonzales v. Raich, 2005*, that the Commerce Clause was originally used to prevent discriminatory state legislation, and that Congress had created its own regulatory authority in the Interstate Commerce Act of 1887 and the Sherman Antitrust Act of 1890. The former was designed to protect farmers from railroad monopolies, and the latter authorized the government to investigate and limit corporate monopolies. The purpose of the Commerce Clause was therefore interpreted to give Congress the authority to prevent corporate monopolies from interfering with competition.

More substantially, between 1778 and 1787, when the colonies were operating under the Articles of Confederation, there was a clause therein reading:

> *Each state retains its sovereignty, freedom, and independence, and every*

power, jurisdiction, and right, which is not by this Confederation expressly delegated to the United States, in Congress assembled.

One main problem with the Articles of Confederation was that states tended to create protectionist trade barriers, a clear impediment to free trade. When the Constitution was written in 1787, they wrote the Interstate Commerce Clause to prevent such barriers and create a nationwide free-trade zone. In other words, to keep trade regular between states.

"The powers delegated by the proposed Constitution to the federal government are few and defined. Those which are to remain in the State governments are numerous and indefinite."

~ James Madison; Federalist Papers #45
Author, Constitution of the United States
Author, Bill of Rights

In addition to explicitly limited and enumerated powers, the Federal Government makes everything it touches worse. These are two great reasons to keep Washington as inconsequential in our lives and businesses as possible. The government's job is to "secure these rights" and that's it.

The Plan

I have reviewed the proposed FY2013 Federal Budget overview and the budgets for every department, and I have identified over a **trillion** in spending that can be cut immediately, which in itself would be enough to balance the budget. Combined with a reform of the tax system, I have calculated a $651B surplus in the first year alone, and increasing each year after that for a decade. At the end of this decade, we would be completely out of debt and could operate at a fraction of the tax rate we have today.

This proposal would eliminate the entire federal tax code and replace it with a flat 17% Sales Tax and a flat 10% Import Tax. The idea thereof is twofold: It would greatly simplify the tax code and eliminate the need for the Internal Revenue Service, and it would motivate companies to bring manufacturing back onto American soil. I do not advocate the Fair Tax, but it has similarities.

This proposal would eliminate all nationalized socialism programs. Unfortunately, a large fraction of Americans have become so utterly dependent on socialized everything that it can't possibly be eliminated all at once. Therefore I have devised a plan to cut them by 10% every year for 10 years, while simultaneously transitioning these programs to the states that want them, and restoring the devastated American manufacturing base. We need to build things again, and we need those people to be building them.

This proposal eliminates all ongoing overseas contingency operations, all foreign aid, six departments, and hundreds of programs within the remaining departments. At the end of the 10 Year Plan, we could eliminate four additional departments. My only goal herein is to show that it is possible to fix our economic crisis, and that to do so we need to get serious about it. Cutting a few billion here and there just won't do it. We need to cut in the trillions. Not surprisingly, the vast majority of the budget is spent on the welfare/warfare state.

This proposal will give us a surplus of over half a trillion in the first year. On the 10th year, we would have a surplus of over $2 Trillion and be completely out of debt. At this point, our federal government outlays would measure under a trillion dollars and the income tax could be slashed to 5%. During these 10 years, additional expenditures would certainly be identified and eliminated, further reducing the needed taxes. The goal is to eliminate the need for both income and Sales Tax altogether. How much money you make is none of the government's business. In this endgame, the remaining constitutionally authorized programs could be paid for once again with other types of taxes and excises only, like they used to be.

I have reviewed Obama's budgets. I have reviewed Paul Ryan's budget, Mitt Romney's plan, and Ron Paul's *Plan to Restore America*. Obama has clearly cut a noticeable amount of fat from the projections of the earlier 2011 budget; but it still puts us hugely in deficit. Ron Paul makes a valiant effort, and puts us in surplus within a few years, but even his plan has a highly noticeable increase in spending over time, and barely returns us to where we were before Obama. Therefore, while Paul's plan would address our immediate problems, none of these plans goes far enough to pay off the National Debt. The only annual increases in outlays should be proportional to the population growth, and even then, only in programs that depend on the size of the population.

We must eliminate the National Debt in order to realize the full economic potential of America; and to do that, we have to get *really* serious. Unlike Paul, I have the advantage of not requiring the approval of the poor and lazy customers of the National Socialism programs, because I'm not planning to be the President of the United States. Therefore, with all marketing and politics safely out of the way, I could create the wondrous Ten Year Plan.

Once the Ten Year Plan is complete and we have a few trillion in the bank (well, in Fort Knox and various secure, secret, military-controlled locations), I would reduce taxes to just slightly above the allocated spending. Every year, we would take the amount on hand, minus a predetermined stockpile for emergencies, and disperse it **evenly among the citizens** in the form of dividends. Think of it as a nice little stimulus package that actually doesn't cost us any money. It's your money, so here, take back what we didn't need. Divide the stimulus amount by the number of citizens, and send that same amount out to everyone equally. When people get an unexpected check, they spend it. Especially so in the lower income brackets.

Let's say one year we have a surplus of $30B. Thirty billion is a drop in the bucket at the federal scale, but divided by 300 million taxpayers, it's a hundred bucks in every pocket. To a lot of Americans, an unexpected $100 is a windfall. Then, obviously, we adjust the tax rate so the surplus isn't so much, since we've long since paid off the debt and accrued what we could call the National Excess. So we give the money back to the people who we took it from in the first place, and it goes right back into the economy; every single year. That's how Stimulus packages **should** work.

For a government that's supposed to be cutting back, reducing the deficit, and balancing its own budgets, I don't see any of that happening. ***Let's get extreme.*** Talk is cheap. Let's look at the actual numbers. Dollars are in billions.

Federal Spending Data

Spending	Obama Budget	Paul Budget	My Budget
2001	1863	1863	1863
2002	2011	2011	2011
2003	2160	2160	2160
2004	2293	2293	2293
2005	2472	2472	2472
2006	2655	2655	2655
2007	2729	2729	2729
2008	2983	2983	2983
2009	3518	3518	3518
2010	3456	3456	3456
2011	3597	3597	3597
2012	3920	3609	2264
2013	4301	2790	2081
2014	4626	2863	1898
2015	4876	2898	1715
2016	5112	3050	1533
2017	5335	3137	1350
2018	5550	3224	1176
2019	5766	3311	1003
2020	5979	3398	829
2021	6216	3485	655
2022	6478	3572	482
2023	6740	3659	482
2024	7002	3746	482
2025	7264	3833	482

Comparison between my plan and other well-known budget plans.

Economic Improvement Projections

Don't be fooled by the media into believing we're recovering from recession. The "improvement" is negligible at best.

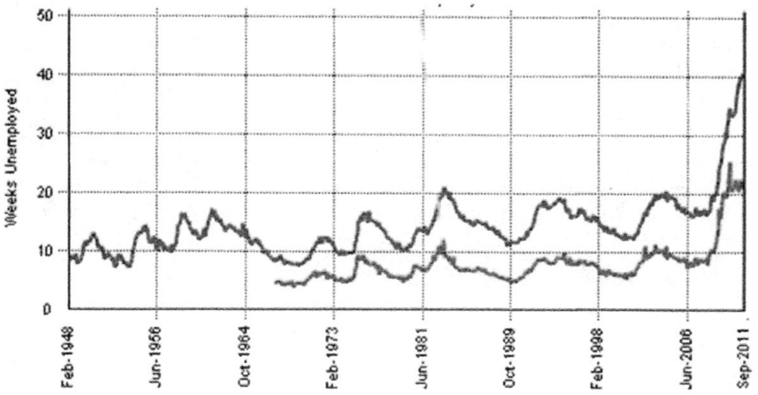

Figure 1 - Duration of Unemployment, 1948 - 2011

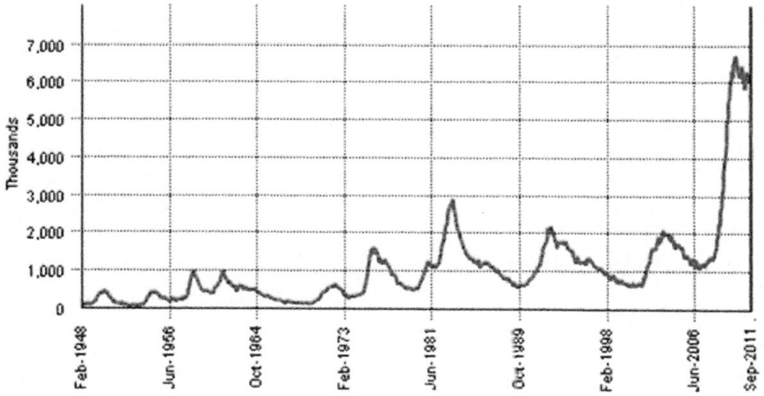

Figure 2 - Unemployed for 27 Weeks and Over, 1948 - 2011

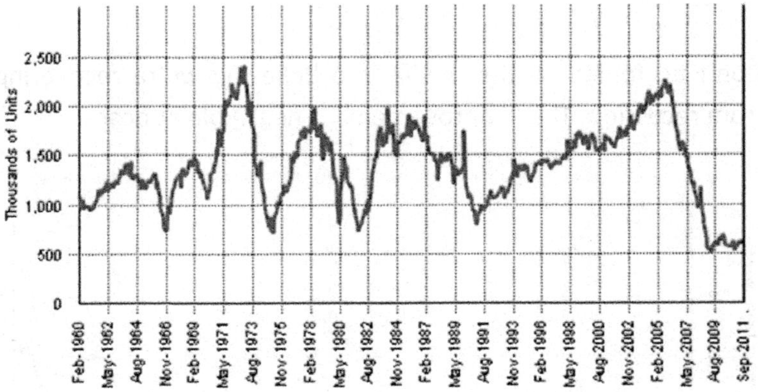

Figure 3 - New Houses Authorized by Building Permits, 1960 - 2011

Jobs Reform

If we want to solve this crisis and restore America to what it was meant to be, we must make Americans self-reliant again. To bring jobs back to America, we must first identify the causes of losing the jobs in the first place.

Contracts - The Federal Government has unconstitutionally bailed out private corporations and voided private contracts between corporations. This is a dangerous violation of contract law. A contract has no value unless both sides trust that contract. As the corporations have no way of knowing whether the government will do it again, they are now choosing to hold onto their money for fear of opening new contracts and having them voided by the government. We must repeal the nullification of these contracts and pass a bill that ensures we will *never do this again*.

Regulation – Every regulation we put on an industry makes it more difficult for that industry to produce its goods and services. We must eliminate regulations, and entire regulatory agencies, in order to simplify the process and streamline what little manufacturing and service industries we have left. Maybe we could even start opening new factories and refineries again.

Legislation – Legislation should only be passed when it directly advances an enumerated power in the Constitution. Every single law that has ever been passed by Congress which does not meet this sole criterion must be repealed. We should legalize the use of all drugs, and allow them to be trafficked as any other products on the market. People should have the right to do to their own bodies whatever they choose to do. This will both reduce the size and scope of government, and introduce entirely new industries and taxable revenue into the economy.

If you don't like drugs, just don't use them. The government is not your keeper; *you* are.

Energy Independence – Drill Texas, Montana, North Dakota, and ANWR, and build new refineries in oil-rich areas that don't have any or enough of them. Renew the railroad system by delivering the refined fuel via railways from oil fields that are far from the coasts. We must produce and refine our own oil domestically, while private companies continue to perform their own research and development of newer and cleaner technologies. We won't be switching to electric or hydrogen vehicles overnight, so we must make ourselves as independent as we can while we wait for the industries and the commensurate demand to catch up to the technologies.

Import Tax – Half of my proposal's new tax code would be a flat import tax on the gross price or value of all goods and services imported into the United States. Obviously, any tax increases revenue, but that's not the purpose of this tax. By taxing importation, we incentivize companies to do their manufacturing in the United States. I would be in favor of exempting raw materials which cannot be produced here, if in turn we increased the import tax incrementally every year until about 90% of goods on the market were "Made in the USA". However, I believe a great deal of those raw materials can be found right here in America. There would also be no export tax; the more we manufacturer and export, the more jobs and the stronger economy we have. An Import Tax has the additional benefit of reducing the price gap between cheap imported crap and expensive American products.

Farm Labor – 53% of all American farm labor is performed by illegal Mexican immigrants. This is a pervasive and well-documented pattern which is costing us **1.325 million jobs**. Each displaced vagrant would introduce one new job for an American citizen to take. It's not great work, but it's work; ideal for teenagers and the grossly unskilled. I would ensure the newly found jobs were advertised nearby. Legalizing drugs would greatly reduce the number of incoming illegals, as well as completely obsolete the underground drug network.

Tax Reform

The current tax code is so convoluted that no tax lawyer or accountant could possibly memorize the entire thing. It's filled with loopholes and imbalances that employ entire industries of jobs that there should be no need for in the first place. With six tax brackets ranging from 10 to 35 percent and a ridiculous number of exceptions, rules, and regulations, it's no wonder companies need to hire entire departments of people to keep track of it all. This overcomplexity forces companies to waste time and money in research and paperwork that could be better spent hiring productive employees and opening new facilities.

My proposal would eliminate the entire federal Tax Code and replace it with two flat taxes: One on all imports, and one on all sales. I've already explained the Import Tax in the Jobs Plan, and it does provide a notable amount of revenue -- especially considering the radical spending cuts -- but the real moneymaker is the flat Sales Tax. No loopholes, exceptions, exemptions, brackets, prebate, or IRS. Nobody would need to file taxes; indeed, the government wouldn't even need to know how much money you make. Everyone could memorize the whole thing in a matter of seconds.

A flat Sales Tax would be enacted on every original sale of any product or service, and could therefore be measured directly against the Gross Domestic Product, much as the Import Tax could be measured thusly directly against the Gross Imports.

The flat Sales Tax would be excised at the final point of sale. The flat Import Tax would be excised at the port, border, or other point of import. While the Constitution authorizes Congress to regulate commerce between the states, there would be no need for them to do so. The only regulation would be at the point of import or final sale.

A flat Sales Tax scales directly in proportion to income. Rich people spend more money than poor people, and would therefore pay proportionately more taxes. The Sales Tax would be paid by the business providing the goods and services; the consumer need not even think about the tax itself. This tax code would be so simple that combined with reduced regulation and legislation, I believe the decreased cost of manufacturing and providing services could entirely offset this paltry 14.5% tax.

A flat Sales Tax includes every single person who buys anything, which could potentially add 100 to 150 million new people to the tax base, thereby allowing an overall lower tax rate. The flat Sales Tax imposes taxes on people who currently do not pay taxes, such as drug dealers, illegal immigrants, the rich, and the poor.

To balance the actual proposed FY2012 budget with this system, we could use either a 14.5% import tax and 14.5% Sales Tax, or no import tax and a 16.2% Sales Tax, and that's before any of my cuts even take effect. I believe the Import Tax to be critical to the Jobs Plan.

The astute observer will realize this plan is technically an increase in gross tax receipts. Consider, however, that it is now spread across nearly a third additional taxpayers. This number could be reduced to as low as 10/14 for the first year to provide a swift boost to the economy and get the jobs rolling along without a deficit. We then follow up with the Ten Year Plan.

I have looked over the Fair Tax; I would prefer it over the present tax code but would not advocate it as the ideal solution.

Its Prebate system is unfair, it taxes excessively, and it deceptively indicates a lower tax rate than it would actually impose. Studies have found it to be indeed neither flat nor fair.

The 16th amendment to the Constitution does not need to be repealed in order to excise these taxes.

> *The Congress shall have power to lay and collect taxes on incomes, from whatever source derived, without apportionment among the several States, and without regard to any census or enumeration.*

Nowhere in this amendment does it say the Congress *must* collect these taxes; therefore, we could eliminate the Income Tax without the need to wait for the repeal process. We could certainly do so, but we wouldn't need to. Article I, Section 8, clause 1 already authorized the Congress to collect taxes:

> *The Congress shall have Power To lay and collect Taxes, Duties, Imposts and Excises, to pay the Debts and provide for the common Defence and general Welfare of the United States; but all Duties, Imposts and Excises shall be uniform throughout the United States*

Section 8 does not specify from where these taxes may be derived, so long as they are "uniform throughout the United States". Therefore both a flat Income Tax and my proposed Import and Sales flat taxes would be constitutional. The 16th amendment was designed to allow a tax to be excised without it being apportioned among the states (Article I, Section 9, Clause

4) or based on the Census results (Article I, section 2, clause 3). With either my flat tax plan or the Fair Tax, this amendment would become obsolete and could be repealed; however, this would not be required to move forward with either plan.

Import Tax ($206B) – Excise on all imports, except raw materials and unique cultural items. Annual imports to the US total $2.239 trillion.

Given that crude oil is currently priced at $103.32 per barrel, we can calculate that we import 1.8 billion barrels per year. Our new oil production having been increased by 8M * 365 = 2.92 billion barrels per year, we no longer need to import any oil.

Given the same 10% tax, and subtracting the obsolete oil imports, we could expect $206 billion in new annual federal revenue while rendering the United States *completely free of all foreign oil dependency.* Perhaps more importantly, American products become relatively cheaper to buy than imported products, thus incentivizing manufacturing, and therefore new jobs.

National Sales Tax ($1.5T) – Excise on all purchases at point of sale across the United States and including international transactions not already otherwise taxed. The Gross Domestic Product is $15.088 Trillion. Given the same 10% tax rate, we could expect $1.5 Trillion in new revenue.

Simplified Tax Code ($121.22B) – U.S. Taxpayers spend more than 7.6 Billion hours annually complying with federal tax requirements. The nationwide mean wage across all job types is $15.95 per hour. Therefore, a simplification of the tax code that eliminates the need to file any taxes could save the United States $121.22 Billion in wasted manpower.

Oil ($29.2B) – Allow private oil companies to set up oil rigs on the continental shelf off the coasts. This is federal territory, but it's water, so there's no state to give it back to. Open a contract with such oil companies which would involve the federal government receiving a small stipend; say $10 per barrel drilled. Require that they leave the water as they found it: Clean up their own spills, and repopulate any species they reduce the population of. Suspend their permit to function thereat upon any violation thereof. Allow states to handle oil companies according to their own laws.

Allow and urge states to allow drilling in their undrilled territory, such as the Arctic National Wildlife Preserve, which has nearly zero wildlife. Let the oil companies and states decide on their own pipeline rules; urge them to build new refineries in oil-rich areas. Eliminate all other federal oil-specific legislation, such as subsidies and regulations.

The USA produces roughly 8,000,000 barrels of oil per day. Given that the drillable space would roughly double, it stands to reason we would potentially add approximately the same amount of production. 8Mbbl * $10 = $80,000,000 daily.

That's $29.2 billion in new annual federal revenue, while roughly *doubling the number of jobs* in the oil industry and the supply of oil. Such increased supply could thereby cut gas prices in half; and that's before we even start cutting regulations and taxes. People might start buying cars and driving for *fun* again!

Given all these new sources of income, and their plentitude, we can eliminate the entire federal tax code, the Internal Revenue Service, and all other taxes that exist today.

Healthcare Reform

Repeal Obamacare, eliminate the Department of Health and Human Services, repeal all healthcare-related legislation, and eliminate all federal healthcare regulations. Let the economy fix itself. Healthcare is a private industry. You have no right to healthcare; what you have is a right to engage in a transaction with a business or individual and try to *buy* healthcare. They have a right to say no.

100 years ago, healthcare was cheap and competition was healthy. People could afford their medication, doctors made house calls, and hospitals didn't make peoples' conditions *worse*. Today, exactly the opposite is true. As the federal government has nested itself deeper and deeper into the healthcare industry, it has become larger, more expensive, and less responsive to patients' needs.

Throughout the course of this gradual and insidious process, the government began to provide healthcare programs to the people through Medicare and Medicaid. Of course, there were strings attached, such as HMOs, giving up your right to choose your own doctor, and the requisite bump in government spending.

Healthcare is a private industry with associated commerce; and the Constitution does not authorize the federal government to interfere in, nor create, industry or commerce. The only authority granted therein is to keep that commerce flowing regularly

Therefore, by getting the government out of the healthcare business, it will become cheaper and its quality will improve.

Ten Year Plan

Unfortunately, as I've described several times in this book, a huge number of people have become utterly and hopelessly dependent on these Socialism programs. Therefore, it would be catastrophic to cut them from the budget altogether and all at once. Due to this, I have instituted a Ten Year Plan to eliminate this Socialist pattern over a period of time, while the programs transition to the states that want them, America recovers from its grossly failed Keynesian dependencies and its citizens learn to run our own lives again.

If we want to solve this crisis and restore America to what it was meant to be, we must get serious about reducing spending. The nationalized socialism programs identified below are by far the largest and most wasteful spending by the Federal Government.

If you want to save for retirement, put your own money into your own retirement accounts. Buy stocks, mutual funds, gold, and silver. If you invest the amount you have been taxed for social security, there would be no difference to your paycheck therefrom, you would know that the money would be there when you're ready to retire, and you would have an average of six times more money upon your retirement.

If you want healthcare when you can't afford it, buy some insurance or save for it while you're healthy. You can get charity from many organizations such as churches and NPOs without forcing it upon others through theft.

If you can't afford to feed and clothe your children, *don't have children*. The ones you have now should be taken from you by state-level Social Services. You are clearly not fit to be a parent and are guilty of child abuse.

If you need money to get by and pay your bills while you're between jobs, save your money while you have a job. If you are physically incapable of performing any work of any kind, then seek help from your local churches, charitable organizations, family, friends, and neighbors. Like our ancestors used to do.

If you got Black Lung Disease from working in a coal mine, then you should have made smarter career choices when you were younger.

None of this is the country's fault. Take responsibility for your own life.

10 Year Sub-Plan

Program	Department	2012 ($M)
Food and Nutrition Service - Supplemental Nutrition Assistance Program / SNAP / Food Stamps	*Agriculture*	$82,232.00
Child Nutrition Programs	*Agriculture*	$18,959.00
Medicare	*Health*	$485,804.00
Medicaid and CHIP	*Health*	$279,049.00
Social Security	*Social Security*	$719,415.40
Unemployment Insurance Administration	*Labor*	$2,958.30
Employment Service / One Stop Career Centers	*Labor*	$849.00
Office of Job Corps	*Labor*	$1,275.00
Unemployment Insurance Benefits	*Labor*	$83,821.

		50
Black Lung Benefits Program	*Labor*	$225.00
Energy Employees Occupational Illness Compensation Program Act	*Labor*	$737.25
Tax Expenditure Program Outlays	*Treasury*	$61,345.50
Total Deferred Socialism ($M)		**$1,736,670.95**

10 Year Sub-Plan

The Proposed FY2012 Federal Budget includes a fair number of uncategorized outlays that I didn't understand well enough to eliminate out of a fear that I might be removing fire extinguishers or security barriers. Therefore, I have categorized those outlays into an accelerated Five Year Plan *within* the Ten Year Plan. Each of these items would be reduced by 20% per year for five years until eliminated completely.

5 Year Sub-Plan

Program	Department	2012 ($M)
Other NFS Activities (NFS)	*Agriculture*	**$561.00**
Other Fire Operations (FS)	*Agriculture*	**$100.00**
Capital Improvement and Maintenance (FS)	*Agriculture*	**$338.00**
All Other (Discretionary)	*Health*	**$51.00**
All Other (Mandatory)	*Health*	**$36,921.00**
All Other (Mandatory)	*Homeland*	**($4,812.00)**
General Legal Activities	*Justice*	**$716.25**
Office of Justice Programs, etc	*Justice*	**$1,482.00**

All Other (Discretionary)	*Justice*	$377.00
All Other (Discretionary)	*Labor*	$326.00
Other International Programs	*State*	$0.00
Guaranteed Loan Commitments	*State*	$0.00
All Other	*Transportation*	$125.00
All Other (Mandatory)	*Treasury*	$8,042.25
All Other	*Veterans*	$1,122.00
Total Known Deferred Waste ($M)		$45,349.50

Year	10YP Savings	5YP Savings	Total Savings
1	$173,667.10	$9,069.90	$182,737.00
2	$347,334.19	$18,139.80	$365,473.99
3	$521,001.29	$27,209.70	$548,210.99
4	$694,668.38	$36,279.60	$730,947.98
5	$868,335.48	$45,349.50	$913,684.98
6	$1,042,002.57	$45,349.50	$1,087,352.07
7	$1,215,669.67	$45,349.50	$1,261,019.17
8	$1,389,336.76	$45,349.50	$1,434,686.26
9	$1,563,003.86	$45,349.50	$1,608,353.36
10	$1,736,670.95	$45,349.50	$1,782,020.45

10 Year Plan – Savings ($M - Excluding outright cuts)

The Ten Year Plan accounts for the reduced spending over each contiguous year between both the Ten Year sub-plan and the Five Year sub-plan to produce incredible results. Here is a table showing the savings from both these plans as a savings per year; not cumulative. Therefore, at the end of 10 years, we would have **reduced the budget by an additional $1.78 Trillion** in addition to the initial across-the-board budget cuts. Even without including the outright cuts, this plan alone would cut **$10 Trillion off the national debt** in a decade.

All things considered, after 10 years, the National Debt would be paid in full. At this point, we have some serious options. We should slash taxes to a bare minimum, eliminate the Federal Reserve, and shift the country back onto the Gold or Silver Standard. Now, the world's richest and most debt-free nation, with incredibly low taxes and regulations and a strong, sturdy currency, we would unleash the full economic potential of the United States of America. Some of that can be done right now.

And that, ladies and gentlemen, is how to fix this country.

I have gone through the entire federal budget and identified hundreds or even thousands of programs which can be safely eliminated. I am currently in the process of transcribing my findings to a form factor suitable for publishing. I estimate the result to be around 1,000 pages in total, which will likely be split into volumes. Then, I intend to move into active executive orders, treaties, and their costs on the economy and liberty. If sales from this booklet justify, I will publish these findings in subsequent books.

I love feedback. Please forward your thoughts to LibertyBook@kconnolly.net or tweet me at @tsilb .

Made in the USA
Monee, IL
04 November 2026

67381312R00036